C000092617

1

For my FFP

For everything

For always.

This is a book about incredible women.

How fortunate that I could learn from the best.

I love you endlessly.

'History's stinking breath in her face'

Carol Anne Duffy, '*Feminine Gospels*'

Contents

Herstory

They found her abandoned

in the receipts.

In the recipes.

In the stitches.

She was the underscore,

the hidden lifeblood

sequestered by

a larger, louder, deeper, richer,

instrument.

She was shivering –

tattered and scrawny.

Diminished in malnourishment,

the underfeeding of her presence

had starved her skinny.

She had been there all along

blinking slowly in the corner.

She was half of every great thankless man.

She had awarded life to every single one of them.

She made him everything he was.

But of course,

no one was looking for her.

Ghostwritten

We are tired of being ghostwriters,

as men claim the credit for our brains.

We did not want to be ghostwriters,

entitling our work with their names.

This is why

millions of us die

with a better idea,

stowed safely away,

inside our heads.

Hatshepsut (1507 BC to 1458 BC)

Hatshepsut declared herself pharaoh and ruled as a man for over 20 years, portraying herself in statues and paintings with a male body and beard. For years, historians referred to her as the 'female king of Egypt'. She married her half-brother, Thutmose II, who inherited the throne from their father, making Hatshepsut his consort. When Thutmose died, she became the regent for her stepson, Thutmose III. They became co-rulers of Egypt, with Hatshepsut becoming the dominant ruler. This was a radical move in Conservative Egyptian society, but she was supported by high-ranking Egyptian officials. Her formal portraits originally combined a female body with male regalia. These became portraits with a male body and false beard. She even claimed that the God Amun was her father and that it was under his divine command that she was intended to take control of Egypt. This artistic conception was not to show things as they were, but as they should be, manifesting and proving in paint that she would become respected as a traditional Egyptian 'king'.

Hatshepsut's reign was a largely peaceful one, and she altered the focus of foreign policy to trade rather than war. However, scenes on the wall of one of her temples show evidence for a short successful military invention in Nubia at the start of her reign. She also greatly augmented Egyptian coffers with a seaborne trading venture to Punt on the African coast, where no Egyptian had been for over 500 years. Restoration and building were also important royal duties which Hatshepsut fulfilled with an extensive construction program. She built numerous temples, but her biggest accomplishment was her Dayr al-Baḥrī temple: her own funerary monument. She was interred in the Valley of Kings, where she extended her father's tomb so that the two could lie together.

Following her death, Thutmose III ruled alone for a further 33 years. At the end of his reign, an attempt was made to remove all traces of Hatshepsut's rule. Her statues were torn down, monuments defaced, and her name removed from the official list of kings, removing the female 'interruption' to the Thutmose succession. Hatshepsut was

obscured until 1822, when the decoding of hieroglyphic script al-
lowed archaeologists to uncover her presence. The discrepancy be-
tween the female name and male iconography caused confusion for
years. Her tomb was found in 1903, when Hatshepsut's legacy as
Egypt's powerful female pharaoh started to be restored.

His Majesty Herself

I built a temple.

Where is he?

They said

I led an army.

Where is he?

They said

I won the gold.

Where is he?

They said

I was found

in the belly of my father;

he had consumed me whole.

King's daughter

King's wife

King's mother

King's self

The woman who was King,

they tried to make me more palatable.

Believable.

So in stone I was man;

in writing was he.

Unendowed but bearded,

swapped softness for savagery,

erased all femininity.

My children will weep when they see me.

Your mother was weak,

I tell them,

I am father now.

Now my head has been shorn,

will you kneel?

Now my breasts have been bound,

will you kneel?

The children I birthed call me father,

now will you kneel?

Found in the belly of my father.

I confounded the archaeologists for years -

they were busy looking for a penis.

Cleopatra (69 BC to 30 BC)

Cleopatra has been remembered as merely the lover of 'great men', and, thanks to Shakespeare, has become the literary and social embodiment of the femme fatale. Cleopatra became queen on the death of her father, Ptolemy XII, in 51 BCE. She ruled Egypt with her two brothers, and, as was customary, likely married her brother Ptolemy XIII. However, he soon had her exiled, leaving him solely in charge. By 48 BC, the Roman Empire was embroiled in Civil War between Julius Caesar and Pompey. When Pompey fled to the capital in Egypt, Ptolemy had him killed. The pharaoh had hoped to win favour with Caesar, but when he arrived, he was furious that a Roman consul had been murdered by a foreign subject.

Cleopatra took advantage of Caesar's displeasure with her brother to endear herself to him. Together, with the force of Caesar's military might, Ptolemy was overthrown and killed. Cleopatra was reinstated as Queen and gave birth to Caesarion ('little Caesar'), although the man himself never declared his paternity. Cleopatra presented herself as the reincarnation of the Egyptian goddess, Isis. For some time, Cleopatra's reign brought a period of relative peace, economic prosperity, and stability to an Egypt which had been bankrupted by civil war. Although she was raised speaking Greek, Cleopatra learnt Egyptian and later only spoke in the native tongue of her subjects.

In 44 BC, Julius Caesar was assassinated, sparking a growing power struggle between Mark Anthony and Caesar's adopted son, Octavian. Despite his marriage to Octavian's sister (Octavia), Anthony commenced a relationship with Cleopatra, and the pair had three children together. Octavian claimed that Anthony was completely enraptured by his new Egyptian Queen, and would give Rome away to Cleopatra. It was seen as a family insult and an affront to Roman honour that Anthony was married to his sister, but having an affair with Cleopatra. This antagonism developed into full-blown civil war, and in 31 BC, Cleopatra joined her forces with those of Mark Anthony to fight Octavian. The pair were decisively beaten in battle, barely escaping back to Egypt. Octavian's forces pursued the couple and captured Egypt's capital in 30 BC. With no chance of a dignified escape, Mark Anthony and Cleopatra both took their own lives, committing suicide on the 12th of August 30 BC. One account of the death has Cleopatra committing suicide by enticing a cobra to bite her. Octavian later had their son, Caesarion, strangled. This ended the Ptolemaic dynasty, rendering Cleopatra the last of all Egyptian Pharaohs.

Many contemporary sources speak of the mystique of Cleopatra's beauty and allure, and many believed that she had in some way bewitched Mark Anthony. Historians have traditionally portrayed Cleopatra's death as an act of shame and cowardice but this is being increasingly interpreted as a political act, preventing her from being humiliatingly paraded around Rome as a prize of the war. Her carefully contemplated suicide allowed her to die on her own terms, as an act of pride and resistance. In Egypt, the Cobra was used to depict female deities, and was culturally important as a symbol of divinity and protection. Therefore, her death by snake bite served as confirmation of her divine and royal status.

Femme Fatale

I lined them up

so that they would fall

into the graves I made them dig.

Efficiency of slaughter.

I smiled –

To each man his own death,

a test, I explained,

as eyes widened in terror,

stretching sockets containing

eyes like olives

almost fell to the floor.

I imagined them bouncing and skidding

over my white marble.

Such a shame the blood will stain.

He screamed as he went.

Won't do –

They will say I was weak.

He spluttered and foamed.

Won't do –

They will say that I cried.

He clutched at his throat.

Won't do –

They will say I fought death.

When the snake bit

his eyes glossed over,

he crumpled neatly

as bare knees thudded –

didn't bruise,

lips remained plump.

I will check back in an hour.

I was choosing the prettiest way to die.

Must preserve the picture,

the beauty, the dignity.

Maybe then,

they will remember me

on my own terms.

Is it my face they see?

When they think of

Egypt's last Queen.

The Six Wives of Henry VIII

Catherine of Aragon (1485 to 1536)

Catherine is remembered for her quarter-century marriage to Henry VIII and her role in sparking the English Reformation during Henry's quest for a divorce from her. She was the daughter of the Spanish warrior Queen, Isabella of Castile, and Ferdinand of Aragon. She was engaged to Prince Arthur in 1502, at the age of three, but he died 5 months into their marriage. Catherine was effectively held prisoner whilst the issue of her dowry was debated. In 1507, she became the ambassador of the Aragonese Crown to England, becoming the first female European ambassador in history.

During her marriage to Henry, Catherine served as regent for 6 months whilst Henry was fighting futile war in France. In 1513, she oversaw a crushing military victory against Scotland at the Battle of Flodden Field. She bore the King's first child, a boy who died 52 days later. She suffered multiple miscarriages and stillbirths, but Mary (later Queen Mary I) was born in 1516. Henry tried to have the marriage annulled, due to his lust for Anne Boleyn as well as his obsessive desire to have a son, claiming that their marriage was invalid in God's eyes due to her previous marriage to his brother.

Catherine remained devout and rejected the claim, as her and Arthur's marriage had not been consummated. The Pope would not annul the marriage and Henry was forced to turn his back on the Catholic Church. She was banished from court and died in 1536. Her daughter Mary was not allowed to visit her or attend her funeral. Catherine never accepted the end of her marriage and died, in her eyes, as England's rightful Queen.

Anne Boleyn (1501 to 1536)

Anne was born in 1501 to Sir Thomas Boleyn and Lady Elizabeth Howard. She spent the majority of her formative years at the French court, returning in 1522. The English court was scandalised by her penchant for French music and fashions. Following a brief affair with her sister, Mary, Henry VIII eagerly pursued Anne Boleyn for 7 years, whilst he was still married to Catherine. Anne refused to become the King's mistress and would not bed Henry until she was married. It is likely that Anne supplied Henry with reformist literature from the continent, which supported his breakaway from the Catholic Church. After sparking the English Reformation to secure the marriage, Henry grew more distant from Anne as it seemed she too would not bear him a son. Anne gave birth to the future Elizabeth I in 1533, but later suffered several miscarriages. Anne was also less willing to accept Henry's infidelities, becoming enraged and jealous when Henry commenced an affair with Jane Seymour. A month after he began courting Jane, Henry had Anne investigated for high treason, and she was sent to the Tower. Anne was found guilty of fabricated charges of adultery, incest and treason. Anne was convicted alongside five men, including her brother, George. Anne was beheaded on Tower Green in May 1536.

Jane Seymour (1509 to 1537)

Despite Henry's infatuation with Anne, Jane is believed to have been his favourite wife. This was almost certainly a conditional love, based on the fact that Jane delivered him a son, the future Edward XI. Jane was not as highly educated as her predecessors, but had a calm and gentle disposition which lent itself to peace-making at court. Jane had served as a lady-in-waiting to the previous Queens, marrying the King just days after the execution of Anne Boleyn. Edward was born in October 1537, but Jane would not live to see him become King. After post-natal complications, Jane died less than two weeks after Edward's birth, aged 29. Jane is also thought to have worked to reconcile her husband with his daughter, Mary, during their marriage. She was the only one of Henry's wives to be given a Queen's funeral; Jane is the wife Henry chose to be buried with upon his own death in 1547. This was, of course, much easier, given the fact that Jane had remained in one whole piece.

Anne of Cleves (1515 to 1557)

Anne was the daughter of the Duke of Cleves and Count of Mark. The marriage to Henry was a political alliance, negotiated by Thomas Cromwell and recommended by Henry's advisers. Henry married Anne in 1540, when she was only just older than Henry's oldest child, Mary. However, Henry had the marriage annulled just six months later, citing the fact that the marriage had not been consummated as well as the fact that Cleves had previously been engaged. Henry blamed the lack of consummation on Anne's appearance, believing himself to have been deceived by her official portrait. Anne's acceptance of the annulment seems to have won her favour with Henry; they became close friends and she was referred to as 'the King's beloved sister'. The failure of the Cleves marriage also provided the excuse for the fall and execution of Thomas Cromwell, the man responsible for negotiating the alliance. Anne lived out the rest of her life with a comfortable allowance and a household at Richmond Palace. Anne, like Jane, had a good relationship with Mary, and reverted back to Roman Catholicism, in line with the new Queen. Anne outlived all of the other 5 Queens, as well as Henry himself. She is the only one of Henry's Queens to have been buried in Westminster Abbey.

Catherine Howard (1524 to 1542)

Henry's new teenage bride was a first cousin of Anne Boleyn. Catherine's early life was extremely turbulent, as one of the many wards of her father's stepmother – the Dowager Duchess of Norfolk. At the age of only 13, her music teacher initiated repeated sexual contact. Later, she became embroiled in an affair with the Dowager's secretary, and was banished to Henry's court to serve as lady-in-waiting to Anne of Cleves. This position was organised by the Duke of Norfolk, Catherine's uncle. Henry was attracted to her youth, beauty and vivacity, and the pair were married in 1540. The spring of the following year, however, Catherine is alleged to have begun an affair with one of Henry's favoured courtiers. By autumn, the rumours had reached the Archbishop of Canterbury, Thomas Cranmer. Cranmer saw this as a chance to reduce the influence of his political rival, Norfolk. He launched an investigation, and Catherine was detained and questioned in 1541. Catherine maintained that the affairs had been non-consensual. In order to find Catherine guilty of a crime, an act was passed making it illegal not to disclose premarital sexual relations to the King. Catherine was executed for high treason at the age of 19, and buried in an unmarked grave at the Tower's parish chapel.

Catherine Parr (1512 to 1548)

Catherine married Henry in 1543, just four months after Howard was beheaded. She would go on to outlive Henry by a year. She had been married twice before, and would marry again shortly after Henry's death, making her the most married English Queen in history. She was also the first Queen of both Ireland and England. Catherine had begun a romantic relationship with Thomas Seymour when she caught the King's eye, but considered it her duty to marry Henry instead. In 1546, the Catholics in Henry's increasingly factional court launched a plot to depose the Protestant Catherine. Officials tried to turn Henry against Catherine, drawing up a warrant for her arrest. Catherine outwitted the plotters, and was reconciled with her husband by shrewdly throwing herself upon his mercy. Catherine was 30 years old when she became Queen – the oldest of Henry's wives and also a scholar. She is the only one of Henry's Queens to have written and published a book in her own name, with 'Prayers and Meditations' in 1545. She was concerned about the lack of religious and scholarly autonomy for women. When Henry died, he left her £7,000 a year to support herself, and ensured she would be recognised as the Queen Dowager. Catherine's final husband was Thomas Seymour, her previous love interest and the uncle of the new King. When they were married, Seymour also displayed an interest in the future Queen, lady Elizabeth. In August 1548, Catherine gave birth to her first child, but died just days later from suspected childbed fever.

Partial to a Catherine

First he tried a Spanish delicacy,
but she became too tough to chew,
unfruitful, bitter, wrinkly -
it was time for something new.

The amuse-bouche, she was next,
but the French feast was saucy.
So he snapped her white neck,
revealing clean bone all could see.

German cuisine was not to his taste,
Anne arrived unappealing.
Thomas too, he went to waste.
By now his stomach was reeling.

His favourite meal was plated,
but the helping was so small,
his appetite unsated,

Jane did not last long at all.

He thoroughly enjoyed her,
gave him a son no less.
But the course went by a blur:
A mouthful and a mess

Rare meat was his next dish,
picked the flesh from his teeth.
Raw flavour for him to relish –
young ones always tasted sweet.

But at the end of the day
he couldn't beat the buffet;
Outlasting him,
there was me –
I'm Catherine number three.

Six courses
the pig.
I wish my parents had named me Margaret.

Artemisia Gentileschi (1593 to 1654)

Gentileschi is the most celebrated female painter of the 17th Century. Her skill was admired across Europe and she was patronised by members of the highest echelons of society, including the Grand Duke of Tuscany and Philip IV of Spain. Artemisia was born in Rome, the eldest of five children and the only daughter of Orazio Gentileschi, under whom she was trained. Her earliest signed painting is entitled 'Susanna and the Elders', and is from 1610. A year later, she was raped by the painter Agostino Tassi, an acquaintance and collaborator of her father. An infamous trial, recorded in surviving documents, ensued in 1612. Tassi was found guilty and banished from Rome, though his punishment was never enforced. After the trial, Gentileschi married a little-known Florentine artist and the pair left Rome for Florence. She had five children, as well as establishing herself as an independent artist. In 1616, she became the first woman to gain membership to the Academy of Arts and Drawing. From 1630, she settled in Naples, where she ran a successful studio until her death.

Following in the footsteps of Caravaggio, her Baroque paintings were some of the most dramatic and dynamic of her generation. She became known for her realism, her accomplished technique, and for placing women and their stories at the centre of all her paintings. Her works present a unique personal perspective on the cultural and social norms of the period, which she often subverted. Using her position as an artist, she was able to comment on the male-dominated nature of society and to place a focus on female agency. This is seen in her chef d'oeuvre – 'Slaying Holofernes', depicting Judith beheading Holofernes. This is inspired by an episode from the apocryphal 'Book of Judith' in the Old Testament, which recounts the assassination of the Assyrian general Holofernes by the Israelite heroine Judith. Many interpreted this as a visual revenge for her rape. Her teenage experience of sexual assault influenced much of her work; themes of abuse of power, rape and violence permeate her paintings. It is likely that these subjects allowed her to process her trauma and leave lasting redress and revenge through her artworks.

Slaying Holofernes

They say I am ruined.

I bring shame to the men.

Damaged property,

it makes them sick to look on me

seeing only where you grasped.

They will not hear how I tried;

how I screamed and flailed to no avail,

he was larger, he was louder,

held the paintbrush with more power.

I snapped mine.

Never wanted to create again.

Disconnected

from my own body.

But it was a crime against my father,

a crime against my virginity –

a mark of quality which he owned.

A purity intact made husbands bid higher.

So they hauled me out to testify

against my father's friend.

The monster he clinked wine with,

father's honour to defend.

All of Rome tutted and whispered to see

a woman so scandalised –

And what about me?

When my very body was the site of the crime,

they were satisfied with five months' exile time.

I wanted your head.

So she put the pain in the paint.

The pain of a million women,

crafting a scene too many had wished.

And she smiled as she painted.

You shall have his head.

Mary I (1516 to 1558)

Mary I was England's first female monarch, ruling for five years between 1553 and 1558. However, Mary's reign suffers from a hangover of Elizabethan propaganda, which casts her as a Catholic zealot, remembered solely for burning 289 Protestants and the embarrassing loss of Calais to the French. Historians have been incredibly harsh about her reign, and only in the 21st century has she begun to receive the revisionism which is deserved.

As the child of Henry VIII and Catherine of Aragon, she was well-educated, and excelled in languages and music. At the age of 6, she was betrothed to Charles V, the King of Spain and the Holy Roman Emperor. The two never married, but Charles remained her lifelong ally. In 1533, Henry divorced Mary's mother and married Anne Boleyn. Mary was demoted and bastardised, forbidden from visiting her mother. Mary was forced to bow to her father's will, for the first and only time in her life, and was forced to deny the Pope's authority, her beloved Mass and her own legitimacy.

When Henry died, her brother, Edward, and his regents advanced a program of Protestant reform, attempting to prevent Mary from attending Mass. After Edward's sudden death in 1553, Mary overcame the attempted coup by the regent Northumberland, launching the only successful military seizure of power in the Tudor period. Her legitimacy won out over the concern about her religious beliefs, and her accession was celebrated on the streets of London.
In 1554, Mary asserted her will over her reluctant council, announcing her intention to marry Philip II of Spain, the son of Charles V. The marriage treaty established that Phillip would have the title of 'King', but none of the powers. This sparked rebellion in the capital but Mary held fast. Tragically, she suffered two 'phantom' pregnancies where she was declared pregnant and secluded, but no child was ever born. Phillip himself found her unappealing and resolved to spend most of his time in Europe. In 1555, Mary revived England's heresy laws and began burning

reformers at the stake, viciously pursuing Archbishop Cranmer. Almost 300 convicted heretics were burned. However, the attempts at currency reform and success in expanding international trade are often overlooked. Mary died in 1558, likely from ovarian cancer. She is buried in the same tomb as her sister at Westminster Abbey, physically overshadowed by Elizabeth in life as well as in death.

Bloody Mary

Bloody Mary, they said
before anyone was dead.
The child inconvenience –
Mother's Catholic head.

When Daddy did it it was okay,
no qualms over man's prey,
burning bodies unbecoming,
of a woman's fragile frame.

Thousands of heads lost their necks,
Protestant, Catholic – who would be next?
Nobody unclefted safe
from Henry's brutal projects.

Wanted to be just like Daddy
while he wished he'd never had me.
Out again, in again, out again, in
your game of succession was tricky.

They hated my husband, my Philip of Spain,

Married him anyway, to England's disdain.

They armed at my choice –

rebellion would not shake my reign.

Love was never taught to me,

you tore the ring from dear mummy

to give to a woman half your age.

Philip's not all I thought him to be.

Thirty-seven years I awaited my turn,

with babes was not blessed although I did yearn.

First Queen Regnant of England and all that you know

is how many stinking reformers I burned.

Amy Robsart (1532 to 1560)

Amy Robsart was born in Norfolk to an evangelical, or, Protestant, family. She was the only child of a substantial Norfolk gentleman. Little is known of her early life, but she was well-educated and wrote well. Three days before her eighteenth birthday, she married Robert Dudley, a younger son of John Dudley – the Earl of Warwick. Evidence suggests that the marriage was a love match. The wedding was celebrated in June 1550, with King Edward IV in attendance.

In 1553, however, Robert Dudley was imprisoned in the Tower of London for his father's role in the attempted accession coup where Northumberland attempted to install Lady Jane Grey on the English throne. After the accession of Elizabeth, he was released from the Tower and became Master of the Horse and a fast favourite of the Queen. Court gossip indicates that the Queen had fallen in love and planned to marry her favoured courtier, should Amy Robsart die from the illness she was suffering in 1558. Rumours grew more sinister, but Elizabeth stayed single and did not choose a foreign suitor to marry.

Amy Dudley lived with her own household in Oxford, and hardly ever saw her husband. When she was just 28, however, in 1560, she was found dead at the bottom of the stairs in Cumnor Palace with a broken neck. The coroner jury's finding was that she had died of a fall down the stairs; the verdict was 'misfortune' – an accidental death. At court, her death caused a scandal, and it was widely speculated that Dudley had orchestrated his wife's demise. For such a prolific social climber, it would be unsurprising that his weapon of choice had been the stairs. He remained Elizabeth's closest favourite, but with this reputation, she could not risk a marriage. Today, historians widely agree that her death was likely a suicide, but some still probe murder scenarios. The medical evidence of the contemporary coroner's report, found in 2008, is inconclusive and is compatible with accident as well as suicide or murder. The 'misfortunate' circumstances of her death remain one of history's mysteries!

Misfortunate Circumstances

My husband was named Robert Dudley,

I was in his way so he shoved me.

The fall broke my neck,

they said wait a sec,

weren't he and the Queen a bit snuggly?

The Mona Lisa (1503 to 1519)

There has been much speculation and debate regarding the identity of the Mona Lisa's sitter. Scholars and historians have suggested numerous possibilities. Most people agree that the sitter was Lisa del Giocondo, the wife of the Florentine merchant – Francesco di Bartolomeo del Giocondo. The style is similar to Renaissance portrayals of the Virgin Mary, featuring a female figure from the waist up. The oil painting is rendered on a poplar wood panel by Leonardo da Vinci, and is probably the world's most famous painting. It was painted sometime between 1503 and 1519, when Da Vinci was living in Florence. It now hangs in the Louvre Museum, Paris, and is visited by millions of people every year. The sitter's mysterious smile and her unproven identity have made the painting a source of ongoing investigation and fascination.

French King, Francis I, acquired the work after the artist's death, and it became part of the royal collection. For centuries the portrait was secluded in French palaces, until revolutionaries claimed the royal collection as the property of the people during the French Revolution (1787–99). After a period of time hanging in Napoleon's bedroom, the Mona Lisa was installed in the Louvre Museum at the turn of the 19th century.

In 1911 the painting was stolen, causing an immediate media sensation. People flocked to the Louvre to view the empty space where the painting had once hung. The museum's director of paintings resigned, and the poet Guillaume Apollinaire and artist Pablo Picasso were arrested as suspects. Two years later, an art dealer in Florence alerted local authorities that a man had tried to sell him the painting. Police found the portrait stashed in a trunk belonging to Vincenzo Peruggia. He and possibly two other workers had hidden in a closet overnight, taken the portrait from the wall the morning of August 21, 1911, and run off. Peruggia was arrested, tried, and imprisoned, while the Mona Lisa took a tour of Italy before making its triumphant return to France.

During World War II the Mona Lisa was singled out as the most-endangered artwork in the Louvre, and evacuated to various locations in France's countryside. It returned to the museum in 1945, but only after peace had been declared. It later travelled to the United States and toured Tokyo and Moscow. In 2022, the Mona Lisa was smeared with cake by a protestor disguised as old woman in a wheelchair. The painting was not damaged, and the widespread media attention garnered drew attention to the climate concerns of the protestor. The Mona Lisa remains the object of media discussion and is still the most visited painting in the world.

Prettier when you smile

When you said, take your hair down
your face is too round,
I did.
When you said, wear brown
your eyes are too dull,
I did.
When you said, cross your arms,
your wrists are too fat
I did.

You have reduced me
to a discontented shrew woman.

You told me to smile,
you look prettier when you smile.

They say my expression is enigmatic,
well, it is thinly veiled disgust.

You cannot paint what you do not know;

You have never made a woman smile.

And look,

now I am in your gallery,

they pay to see me hung

among the treasures of the world.

I remind you

that you do not have control.

You can build planes,

you're a pain.

You can paint,

what a saint.

You calculate,

isn't he great?

They say you are a genius,

But you cannot make me smile.

No equation will tauten the muscles of my mouth

into the curve you desire.

It is how I retain power.

and it is proof.

We've been telling women they look prettier when they smile

for centuries.

Elizabeth I (1533 to 1603)

Elizabeth was the last Tudor monarch; the daughter of Henry VIII and Anne Boleyn. Her early life was full of uncertainties, and her chances of succeeding the throne seemed slim after her half-brother Edward acceded. Her early life was also marked by the trauma of child abuse from Thomas Seymour, who often visited Elizabeth's bed chambers and made advances in the hopes of furthering his political career. The ensuing scandal abruptly thrust Elizabeth into the harsh reality of the adult world. She was third in line to the throne behind her Catholic sister Mary, and only narrowly escaped execution following a plot to overthrow Queen Mary in 1554.

Elizabeth succeeded to the throne after Mary's death in 1558. She was well-educated, fluent in five languages, intelligent, determined and shrewd. Her forty-five-year reign is generally considered to be one of the most glorious in English history. Elizabeth established a secure Church of England, a pragmatic compromise between Roman Catholicism and Protestantism. Her reign also saw many 'voyages of discovery', including those of Francis Drake and Walter Raleigh. Such expeditions prepared England for an age of colonisation and expansion, laying the foundation for the British Empire with the establishment of the East India Company in 1599. Arts in England also reached what is considered to be their highest point, with artists, architects and theatres thriving. Her reign encompassed the ascendancy of Shakespeare; she attended the first performance of 'A Midsummer Night's Dream'.

Elizabeth never married, which ended the Tudor dynasty, and she was hailed by adoring citizens as 'Gloriana', 'Good Queen Bess' and 'The Virgin Queen'. Elizabeth presented this decision as a choice for the good of the nation, in order to avoid a scenario where England became merely a European satellite for the homeland of Elizabeth's husband. Instead, she claimed she was married to the nation. Such rhetoric as this, exhibited in her dazzling speeches, won over the vast majority of her subjects.

However, the reign was also marked by turmoil in foreign policy. Mary Queen of Scots, seen as a likely successor to Elizabeth, was the focus of rebellion and assassination plots. Under Elizabeth, Mary would spend nineteen years a prisoner before her eventual execution in 1587. The foreign situation was also deeply unstable, as religious differences in Europe provided the excuse for a Spanish Invasion. In 1588, aided by a combination of luck and skill, the English Navy defeated a Spanish invasion fleet of around 130 ships. The defeat of the 'Spanish Armada' was lauded in propaganda as proof of England's superiority in Europe. Wars and economic depression had also scarred the country, and left Elizabeth's Stuart successor with huge debts.

Overall, however, Elizabeth deftly guided England through a period of great danger, both internally and abroad. She died at Richmond Palace in March 1603, having become a legend in her lifetime. The date of her accession was to become a national holiday for the next two hundred years.

Mrs England

You reached for a child's body

with a man's hand.

You found me when I was smooth, unmarked,

and didn't know danger

when it came to my bed in the dark.

You found me when I had flesh unkneaded -

Innocence coloured you a friend

So I said I was wedded to England.

It was easier to wed her.

She didn't steal a girlhood

which wasn't hers to take.

She was kinder

than a man.

And when they demanded to know why

I never picked a husband,

was it really a wonder?

I did not cry when he was beheaded.

Instead, consecrated body and heart

to the nation.

Watched the Council as they fretted

I wouldn't pick a man to wed.

I knew that if I didn't choose one,

My bed would stay my bed

You picked me as prey,

thinking I was weak.

But I will end a dynasty

and be buried with my head.

Anne Hathaway (1556 to 1623)

Anne Hathaway (the original, not the actress!) grew up in Shottery, a village close to Stratford-upon-Avon. She grew up in the farmhouse which was the Hathaway home, since her father was a yeoman farmer. He died in 1581, leaving Anne with a modest dowry. In her father's will, her name is listed as 'Agnes'. Anne married William Shakespeare when he was 18. She was 26 years old and already pregnant with their first child. To avoid scandal, it was essential that the couple married before signs of the pregnancy became too obvious. Following the wedding, Anne moved in with William and his parents, into their family home on Henley Street.

The pair had three children: Susanna and twins Hamnet and Judith. Hamnet died at the age of 11 during one of the frequent outbreaks of the bubonic plague. Very little is known about Hathaway, or indeed her relationship with Shakespeare. For most of their married life, Shakespeare lived in London, writing and performing his plays while she remained in Stratford. Although he took other lovers in London, he returned to Stratford for a period every year and chose to live out his life in retirement from the theatre with his wife in Stratford, not in London. Shakespeare died in 1616, and Hathaway outlived him by 7 years. Upon his death, Shakespeare left his 'second best bed' to Anne in his will. Anne Shakespeare died in 1623.

The Playwife

When you are gone,

I collect the iambs

you have dropped

around the house.

You were always careless

With your things.

These ones are heavy;

I feel in them the weight

of the things you will not say to me.

Oh the twisted irony!

The pre-eminent playwright

makes grown men cry,

extracting the tears of audiences across the land.

But the wife is not privy

to the innards of the husband with

the most emotive mind of our time.

My emotions do not reward you as the stage does,

so you leave me, Londonbound.

Saving up all of your feeling for the page -

You take our trauma, make it prance on the stage

And now you are gone.

Leaving me, alone,

with your unresolved iambs

and your second best bed.

Me too, *Shakespeare*

Times really do not change
Hundreds of years but still the same
I'll warrant her, full of game
I bet, she's really good in bed

Look in her eyes, she definitely wants it
Methinks it sounds a parley to provocation
Well, she dresses as a temptation
Bare legs, bare shoulders, too short, cut low
Why do they see sex in how I dress?
In my very anatomy, yours to possess?

But men are men
Sounds familiar
Boys will be boys I guess
Maybe we wouldn't need the saying
If it happened less
Didn't see 'yes'
In a short dress

He was drunk he didn't know any better

Men put an enemy in their mouths to steal away their brains

But don't tell anyone, please, rape's a mark that stains

Keep it inside - you have his promising career to think of…

He was just trying to have fun, he's a party animal

Revel, and applause, transform ourselves into beasts

It was her own fault that she drank too much, but

You or any man living may be drunk at some time,

She should have some more self-control,

　　　　　　　some modesty,

　　　　　　　some shame,

accept blame.

And *he* is still the hero of the story

Nadezhda Alliluyeva (1901 to 1932)

As a two-year-old in 1903, Alliluyeva was supposedly saved from drowning by the visiting twenty-five-year-old Stalin. When he was staying in St. Petersburg, Stalin often lodged with the Alliluyeva family. Evidence suggests that he may have had an affair with Olga Alliluyeva (Nadezhda's mother and his future mother-in-law). In March 1917, Stalin returned to St. Petersburg, now Petrograd, to join the momentum following the February Revolution and the overthrow of Tsar Nicholas II. Nadezhda was now sixteen, and fell in love with the striking revolutionary.

After the October 1917 Revolution, Nadezhda became Stalin's personal assistant as he embarked on his new role as Commissar for Nationalities, living with him throughout the Russian Civil War. Stalin had been married before, but his first wife, Ekaterina Svanidze, died in 1907 from typhus. Stalin married Nadezhda in 1919 and the pair had two children. After the civil war, they returned to the Capital, where Stalin prevailed in the power struggle following Lenin's death. She found life in the Kremlin incredibly suffocating and did not enjoy motherhood. Her husband, who she had once believed to be the archetype of the Soviet 'new man' had turned out to be unstable and prone to violent mood swings. Stalin turned out to be a quarrelsome bore, often drunk and flirtatious with the wives of his colleagues.

In 1929, bored of being cooped up in the Kremlin, Nadezhda enrolled on a chemistry course and diligently attended university by public transport, shunning Stalin's official limousine. Her new-found student friends, not knowing who she and her husband were, told her horrific storied concerning Stalin's collectivisation policy. She confronted Stalin, accusing him of 'butchering the people'. Stalin responded angrily and had her friends arrested. Days before her death, Nadezhda confided to a friend that 'nothing made her happy'.

On the evening of November 8th 1932, Stalin and Nadezhda hosted a banquet to celebrate the fifteenth anniversary of the October Revolution. The pair regularly argued; this evening was not different. Nadezhda accused Stalin of being inconsiderate; he responded by humiliating her in from of their guests, flicking cigarettes at her and verbally abusing her. Nadezhda stormed out, and Molotov's wife walked with her around the Kremlin grounds until she had calmed down and retired to bed. The following morning, servants found her dead – she had shot herself with a pistol. The rumour was that Stalin had killed her, as the unhappiness of their marriage was not a secret. Nadezhda left Stalin a note, attacking him on both personal and political grounds. Stalin took the death badly, believing she had taken her life to punish him; he did not attend her funeral or visit the grave. The public was told that Nadezhda had died of appendicitis, her daughter only found out the truth a decade later by mistake. On the day of her funeral, Stalin commented that 'she went away as an enemy'.

SAGs (Socialists and Girlfriends)

I loved you like I love the Revolution.

We were drunk on vodka and Marxist theory

I fell for the romantic revolutionary

who, in bed, whispered sweet leninisms to me;

Our love was stained red and

I clung to you, clutched fast your sweep of inky black hair

as you thrashed, battered, schemed, murdered

your way through politics.

If communism was a game - you'd won;

Your rules changed every day.

I followed you to the top but

the Kremlin is boring -

even though we filled it with children,

You and I.

It is mostly I now.

It is a glass house of light-treading

I fear I will shatter -

hard to be the Dictator's darling

Our babies were the product of violence,

of revolution.

They are tiresome screaming things,

Daddy's raging temper.

I raised them to the sound of spilled blood;

When you reach for them,

you stain their downy heads with bloody hands.

Fellow Soviets fall as the country tears itself apart

for your cause.

It is one I do not recognise;

Your hair is flecked with grey now

Now at dinner

you draw up lists of people to kill.

Friends who dined with us yesterday;

You wonder why I have lost my appetite.

Thinking of human flesh

doesn't put you off your beef.

Now in bed

they are not my limbs

draped over yours.

You whisper in the dark

into the skin of another.

You smell of new women every week.

Your friends think I am mad,

I think that they are crude.

I smile at them at dinner

knowing you have fucked their wives.

They should act wisely,

I know they are on tomorrow's menu.

On the fifteenth anniversary

of the revolution,

you joke, base as usual,

but I am transfixed by the hands

that once caressed

now sign citizens to their deaths.

You do not touch me anymore

I fear the blood would contaminate me.

I cannot stop staring at your hands;

Your hair is mostly grey.

They will think that you did this.

You are the one I blame;

I tell you so in a note,

dripping with contempt.

You are weak as a husband and a ruler,

fear your only tool.

My finger pulled the trigger,

but on your head the blame.

You tell them,

My wife died of appendicitis:

It is easier to swallow.

At least your image is intact,

unlike your wife's head.

The propaganda machine whirs -

Mrs Stalin was sick.

You say I went away an enemy.

I wish I had known sooner

you would butcher me

as well as Russia.

History Repeated

What happens when you unmake a law

and set a country back a century?

Will it gather momentum?

Repeal five waves of women's wars?

Will we explain to our children how

first they took away abortion;

then they took our contraception;

next they took away our votes.

Now we are gatherers again,

merely watching the men hunt.

It did not take long

before we were back at original sin.

If only Eve hadn't eaten that apple.

Beware the man who believes

that life was better in the fifties

and wields the law to actualise

his delusion.

And so we will wait,

with hands pressed to the glass,

cold to touch; ever-unbudging.

The whorls of our fingertips

become fleeting impressions

on the fogging surface.

Pummelling and battering has no effect;

Our pounding diminishes,

falls limp to the ground,

drifting and settling like an echo.

It lands softly on the pile of pleas

which clamoured then fell from deaf ears.

It takes over a million years for glass to
decompose.

I am not hopeful.

.

Printed in Great Britain
by Amazon

26229802R00036

how to fall in love with yourself

HOW TO FALL IN LOVE WITH YOURSELF

An Hachette UK Company
www.hachette.co.uk

Vie Books, an imprint of Summersdale Publishers Ltd
Part of Octopus Publishing Group Limited
Carmelite House
50 Victoria Embankment
LONDON
EC4Y 0DZ
UK

www.summersdale.com

Printed and bound in China

ISBN: 978-1-78783-934-2

Substantial discounts on bulk quantities of Summersdale books are available to corporations, professional associations and other organizations. For details contact general enquiries: telephone: +44 (0) 1243 771107 or email: enquiries@summersdale.com.

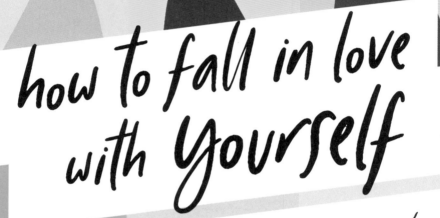

how to fall in love with yourself

a self-acceptance journal

Anna Barnes

vie

Contents

Introduction

We all strive to be better versions of ourselves. But while self-improvement can be a positive thing and make us feel good, when things don't go to plan – or we believe we've failed in some way – we often beat ourselves up about it. This can lead to low self-worth and poor mental health, and a general feeling of meh!

It's time to start thinking about ourselves differently. What if we accepted ourselves, just as we are – with all our perceived faults and shortcomings? What if we actively embraced everything from our wobbly bits to our funny quirks? Imagine how that would feel for a moment. Ask yourself what it might be like to believe in yourself wholeheartedly, and to love yourself completely. Self-acceptance is both freeing and vital. Imagine what you could achieve without your inner mean girl telling you that you're not good enough, or ready, or deserving? The sky really would be the limit.

This book will be your guide on your journey to self-acceptance, offering practical ways to boost self-worth and reach for the life you always imagined as you fall totally in love with yourself.

Rules to live by

THERE IS NO RIGHT
WAY TO LOOK AND
THINK AND FEEL

YOU ARE
EXACTLY WHERE
YOU NEED TO
BE, RIGHT NOW

YOU ARE
BEAUTIFUL,
JUST AS
YOU ARE

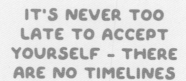

Cut out this page and repeat these mantras every morning – because they're all true!

How to use this book

This book offers a mix of tips-based advice and activities. The techniques are a mix of holistic therapies, such as mindfulness and grounding exercises, as well as the more formal therapies used by psychologists when treating anxiety or low mood, like Cognitive Behavioural Therapy (CBT). It's best to read it from cover to cover and then dip in to the activities that resonate with you. There is no "one size fits all" approach to self-acceptance and that's the main message of this book – we are all unique and we are all wonderful!

Chapter One

THE IMPORTANCE OF SELF-LOVE

INTRODUCTION

Think about your closest relationships for a moment. What thoughts come to mind when you see or think of these special people in your life? It's highly unlikely that you focus on perceived negative traits – the things that make them different to you or the societal norm – though, in fact, these differences are often what make them the people you love and care about in the first place. Now, imagine seeing yourself through the eyes of a loved one – quirks, faults and all – and liking and accepting what you see: this is self-love.

Loving yourself begins with being kind to yourself and making more time for the things that you enjoy – the stuff that makes life really worth living. It's about allowing yourself to bloom and seek out what makes you truly happy. It's also about self-forgiveness when things aren't so great, and being aware of when you need to regroup and try again. It's also about standing up for what you believe in and saying no to the things that sap your self-worth.

This chapter shows you the ways to see the best in you.

YOU ARE BEAUTIFUL: EMBRACE IT. YOU ARE INTELLIGENT: EMBRACE IT. YOU ARE POWERFUL: EMBRACE IT.

Michaela Coel

WHAT SELF-CARE MEANS

"Self-care" refers to any deliberate act you undertake that protects and nurtures your own physical, mental, emotional and spiritual health. It's not some woo-woo nonsense and it's not a luxury that you must earn or deserve; it's vital to your well-being and should be taken seriously! Self-care encompasses many things, from eating well and exercising to becoming more aware of your mental well-being and the importance of rest. When we take care of ourselves we feel energized and more connected in our relationships and our passions. When we feel good in ourselves, we do good things and good things happen.

Often the biggest barrier to self-care is guilt. Feeling bad about spending time tending to your own needs is common, especially if you feel you should be caring for someone else or doing something that appears outwardly more productive. But remember, taking time to look after your own mental and physical well-being will ultimately leave you with more reserves of energy and a more positive outlook for everything else too. It's time to be kind to yourself. What kind things can you do for yourself today?

Acts of kindness to myself

Have you told you lately that you love you?

DON'T BE HARD ON YOURSELF

Part of being kind to yourself is recognizing that everyone makes mistakes – they're a part of life and they often teach us something valuable about ourselves. So next time things go wrong, don't give yourself a hard time about it. Instead, accept what has happened. Make sure you are accountable and apologize if necessary, then forgive yourself fully. Learning from mistakes and moving on is far healthier than continually berating yourself and feeling guilty for evermore.

Try this exercise in forgiveness. It's called the Empty Chair Technique, and it's often used to help experience empathy for the other person ... but in this case the other person is you. Imagine you are sitting across from yourself (it gets easier the more often you try it!); describe your feelings toward this other you about the mistake they have made or their perceived failing. Now sit in the chair of this other you, and reply to what you have just said. Respond with empathy and compassion, and see if you can fully forgive yourself. Cultivating forgiveness and acceptance in this way not only benefits your psychological and physical health, but it will ease this invisible pressure of your inner critic going forward.

WRITE A FORGIVENESS LETTER TO YOURSELF

Another way to heal inner conflict is to write a letter to yourself. Begin by addressing the things that may have caused upset or disappointment. Explain how these things affected you and the feelings that you experienced. Next, write how you wish things had been dealt with differently and the outcomes that you hoped for. Finish off the letter by forgiving yourself, offer kind words and empathy and say that you will learn from this experience and not berate yourself any more.

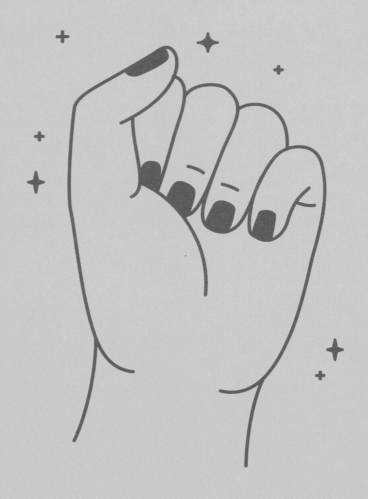

Forgiveness does not change the past, but it does change the future.

Anonymous

THE LITTLE THINGS

The little things can so often be the big things. Reward yourself every day with one or more favourite simple pleasures. It could be getting up early to write a page of your diary, going for a walk and listening to the birds, or snuggling under the duvet and reading a chapter of a book – whatever makes you feel good. Deliberately undertaking these little moments will fill you with happiness.

Make a list of your favourite small, simple pleasures, and then plan to include them in your day-to-day life.

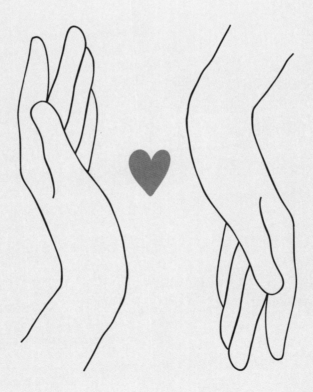

SLOW DOWN AND
SET YOUR OWN PACE

To help build a healthier attitude toward yourself, another important thing to do is to simply slow down! Many of us live at a faster pace than is comfortable as we try to juggle a whole range of commitments and demands on our time. This can leave us feeling stressed when we need to apply the brakes, for instance when we have to wait for something or we're too unwell to continue at our usual breakneck speed. Combat this frustration by using these pockets of time to relax; try some deep breathing, stretching, listening to soothing music or simply gazing out of the window.

A study published in *Psychological Science* magazine suggests that taking time out of your day to just sit and chill out will increase your commitment to your goals and productivity.

Another study published by the University of Central Lancashire found that when we allow ourselves to daydream, our problem-solving capabilities improve and we become more creative in our thinking. So, try to schedule in time to let your mind wander! One fun way to do this is to simply doodle with a pen and paper – use the blank page to take a pen for a walk and watch ideas form in front of you!

NOBODY'S PERFECT, SO GIVE YOURSELF CREDIT FOR EVERYTHING YOU'RE DOING RIGHT, AND BE KIND TO YOURSELF WHEN YOU STRUGGLE.

Lori Deschene

Every day is precious
and full of hope

Life isn't rosy for anyone all the time, and when things seem bleak we often turn to our friends or family, but the most important person to have on your side is you. Showing yourself some love and reminding yourself that good times will come is vital. Cultivating hope for the future can really help ease feelings of fear and worry about what might lie ahead. The psychological benefits of being hopeful include a greater resilience when faced with adversity and the ability to recover more quickly when negative things happen in your life.

Here's something simple you can do to have a permanent reminder of happier times that you can disappear into when you need to feel more hopeful. When something funny, cute, memorable, silly, crazy or hilariously funny happens, write it down on a strip of paper and pop it into a jar with a screw-top lid. You'll be amazed how quickly the jar fills up with precious moments. When you need a boost, just pick out a slip of paper and soak up the nostalgia.

Another way to feel more hopeful is to share other people's hopes and even borrow hope from the more optimistic people in your life. Write down the names of the people that you love and trust implicitly when you are feeling fragile. Include their phone numbers so the information is all there whenever you need it. Having these safe relationships in which you can be vulnerable and speak your mind is essential to a positive and hopeful outlook.

YOU'RE GOING TO BE OK. BETTER THAN OK. YOU'RE GOING TO BE GREAT!

Reese Witherspoon

Chapter Two

FOCUS ON WHAT'S GOOD FOR YOU

INTRODUCTION

How do we know what's good for us and what we should think, feel, say and do? Do we learn this from parents, school, peers? From what we read or see on screen? Or from all of the above? It's certainly a conundrum that has become all the more difficult due to the constant bombardment of points of view, standards, morals and general information overload we experience these days. Sifting through the junk to discover our true selves and what's good for us can be like searching for that proverbial needle in a haystack. It can lead us to feeling like we're treading water and not really going anywhere.

Not knowing what to do with your life or what to do next can hit you at any age. But it doesn't mean you're a lost cause (although it can feel like it). This chapter will help you to navigate your way out of the brain fog and get moving in the right direction toward a happy and fulfilled life.

GOOD STUFF/BAD STUFF

Lists are a great way to bring clarity to your thoughts and help find a clear path to sustained happiness. Writing a list of the good and bad things in your life can be cathartic and revealing. Try it out here. Remember, this is your journal so you can write whatever you want – don't let any niggling worries about what other people might think try to alter your view on what's good for you – this is for **you**.

When you have finished your list, rate each thing out of ten and then order them by score to give you a Top Ten of the best things in your life and a Top Ten of the worst things in your life.

What would your life be like if you had more of the best things and fewer of those bad things?

Ask yourself: are those bad things useful? (There will always be things in our lives that we are not keen on but are necessary or good for you all the same.)

And if they're not, can you drop them? Self-care is about recognizing the things that aren't working, the things that drain you, or the things that have just hung around and you've brushed to the side for too long. It's time to deal with those things, and live the life you've always dreamed of.

Good Stuff	Score	Bad Stuff	Score

Good Stuff	Bad Stuff
1	1
2	2
3	3
4	4
5	5
6	6
7	7
8	8
9	9
10	10

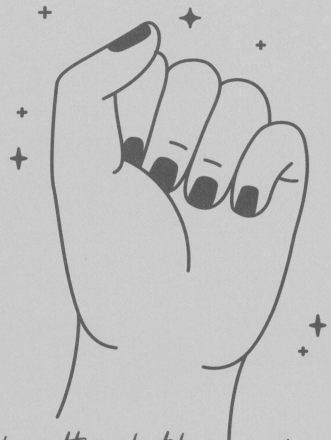

No matter what has gone before,
you can always take a fresh
step into a hopeful future.

Anonymous

Give + take =
a sense of belonging
and self-worth

Think of self-love as though it's a plant needing to be nourished and nurtured. A little watering and loving care each day helps the plant to flourish and maintain its strength and longevity. In exactly the same way, self-love needs tending to help it grow and bloom. And it can't be done in isolation; fulfilment so often comes from helping others, building relationships and being part of a supportive, like-minded group. Sharing your skills with others, providing an empathetic ear to someone in need, or simply volunteering your time to a good cause, can all help to grow your self-love and feelings of goodwill in your life as a whole. Research has shown that people who help others have improved self-worth and even live longer!

What acts of kindness could you do for others today? Think about the people in your life who would appreciate a phone call, a funny meme or a small pick-me-up, whether it's a compliment, a home-made gift or a bar of their favourite chocolate. Little things can really make a big difference. Reach out to your friends and family and feel your self-love soar.

LETTING GO OF NEGATIVE EMOTIONS

We all have a habit of holding on to negative emotions, guilty feelings and regrets. It's time to hit delete on those negative thoughts, so you can move forward to a happier, brighter future. Sometimes it feels good to say, "No more!" and banish the bad thoughts once and for all. Start your campaign here:

I'm saying NO to...

Bye Bye to...

Never again to...

See ya!

Once you have let go of
past disappointments
and upsets, you are ready
to embrace change.
Your new future awaits!

We set the standard of how we want to be treated. Our relationships are reflections of the relationships we have with ourselves.

Iyanla Vanzant

BE UNAPOLOGETICALLY YOU

So now you've put the trash in the trash, it's time
to revel in what makes you **you**, and follow your own
yellow brick road to happiness. Don't feel under pressure
to do or be what others expect of you – because no
one knows you better than you know yourself.

Fill in these inspiration bubbles with activity ideas
that will make you happy – one step toward
realizing happiness is writing it down.

Celebrate
your uniqueness

Being your authentic self means living for you rather than for or through anyone else. It's about forging your own path and living up to your own expectations, rather than those imposed upon you. But where do you start? It doesn't always come naturally, as we worry that the world won't accept us if we are true to ourselves. In a recent study by psychologists on self-awareness, the results showed that only ten per cent of us are self-aware and therefore in alignment with our true selves. How can this number be so low? Are we all too scared to express ourselves? It would seem so. So how do we change that? This is where self-acceptance comes in – when you love and accept yourself fully, and embrace the fact that you are perfectly imperfect, you can begin to celebrate your wonderful self.

Here are some affirmations to live by:

- ♥ I am true to my values.
- ♥ I will not shy away from speaking my mind.
- ♥ I will seek support when I need it.
- ♥ I admit my mistakes and they won't stop me from reaching for my dreams.
- ♥ I am guided by what is important to me.
- ♥ I know my strengths and I am proud of every one.
- ♥ I say no to the things that sap my energy and happiness.
- ♥ I feel all my feelings.

I DON'T FOCUS ON WHAT I'M UP AGAINST. I FOCUS ON MY GOALS AND TRY TO IGNORE THE REST.

Venus Williams

STOP LOOKING AT OTHERS AND THINKING, "I WANT WHAT SHE'S GOT!"

Continually striving for perfection, which in itself is an impossible goal, will prevent you from being happy and deny you the opportunity to feel good about everything you have achieved. One of the most common traits of perfectionism is comparing yourself with others – feeling inferior because someone has a better job, a bigger house or more money than you... the list goes on! This steers you away from looking at all the positive things happening in *your* life. Everybody is on their own journey; we can only try to be the very best versions of ourselves.

Take the opportunity to recognize and list what you are good at, and areas in your life that could be improved. Writing these things down can help you to see where you are on your own journey – how far you've come, and where you want to go next.

Hey, I'm great at all these things!

And I'm going to strive to be great at these things too:

Chapter Three

LOVE THE SKIN YOU'RE IN

INTRODUCTION

How many of us have looked in the mirror and not liked the shape or size of the person staring back at us? How many of us have wished our complexion was a bit clearer, or that our hair was a bit thicker, or our teeth were a bit whiter?

The truth is, we live in a society which has trained us to be dissatisfied with our appearance. Not only are we regularly confronted with images of picture-perfect bodies, but we are also told that we need certain products in order for us to fix our "imperfections".

Well, here's the good news: you're perfect as you are. Your body shape, your skin colour, the length of your limbs – these are all the things that make us unique. There is only one of you, in this entire universe, so why would you want to waste any of your time trying to look like someone else, or be someone else's version of beautiful?

This chapter will explore ways in which you can nurture and respect your body, and offer you practical tips and advice to give it what it needs to thrive. With useful ideas and methods to become more in tune with yourself – such as meditation and mindfulness practices – you'll soon learn how to help yourself feel your best.

It's time to stop finding faults with your body, and start falling in love with it.

Check in
with yourself

Take a moment now to really think how you feel about your body. What perceptions do you have about yourself?

Now think about *why* you might feel the way you do about your body. If you feel negatively toward the way you look, can you think of any reasons for your dissatisfaction? Do you remember a time when you were content with your appearance?

Though these exercises may not be comfortable for you, working out what you feel about your body and why you feel this way is an important step in overcoming negative self-talk. The next important step is to reframe the thoughts you have about yourself.

To start developing a more positive mindset, try writing down three physical and three non-physical things you like about yourself, and taping your list up somewhere you look every day (like a bathroom mirror). Repeat these things to yourself daily, both when you wake up and when you're about to go to sleep.

You could also evaluate your negative thoughts when they appear in your mind, and try to cast them in a different light. If, for example, you dislike your stretch marks, try instead to marvel at the way your skin has allowed you to grow. Your body can do incredible things, and you should focus on all the ways it can help you to dance, eat, laugh and enjoy your life – not how it looks while doing so!

EMBRACE WHAT MAKES YOU UNIQUE, EVEN IF IT MAKES OTHERS UNCOMFORTABLE. I DIDN'T HAVE TO BECOME PERFECT BECAUSE I'VE LEARNED THROUGHOUT MY JOURNEY THAT PERFECTION IS THE ENEMY OF GREATNESS.

Janelle Monáe

MOVE YOUR BODY

We are surrounded by messages which reinforce the idea that fitness means being super slim and toned – so it's no wonder that so many of us see exercise simply as a way to reach an aesthetic goal. But fitness is so much more than this, and moving your body can bring many more benefits than just an "ideal" body shape.

Research shows that physical activity can not only lower your risk of developing certain health conditions, but can also boost your mood, improve your self-esteem, better your sleep quality and reduce your risk of stress and depression.

Whether you go for strengthening, stretching or aerobic exercise, make sure to choose a way of moving that you enjoy. Exercise doesn't have to be a chore – it should be something you look forward to. Try out lots of different workouts and see what works best for you. It could be dancing around your living room, jogging around the park, doing yoga with friends or swimming in the sea – just find something that makes you feel alive.

If starting to exercise feels a bit daunting to you, remember that it can be as simple as going for a walk; even a simple 30-minute walk each day can improve your health and well-being, and should be fairly easy to fit into your existing schedule. And not only will being outdoors lift your spirits, but the exercise itself will release endorphins to boost your mood – a definite win–win.

Remember: movement can make you happy!

MOVING EVERY DAY

This month, challenge yourself to get moving every day – even if that only means going for a short walk or doing some yoga at home. Track your activity level on the chart below, and on the following page, record your mood. At the end of the month, see if you can find any correlation between your activity level and your emotions – do you feel any happier on the days you're more active?

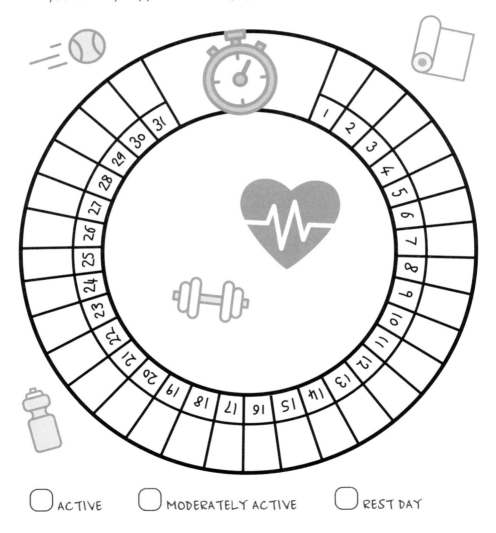

○ ACTIVE   ○ MODERATELY ACTIVE   ○ REST DAY

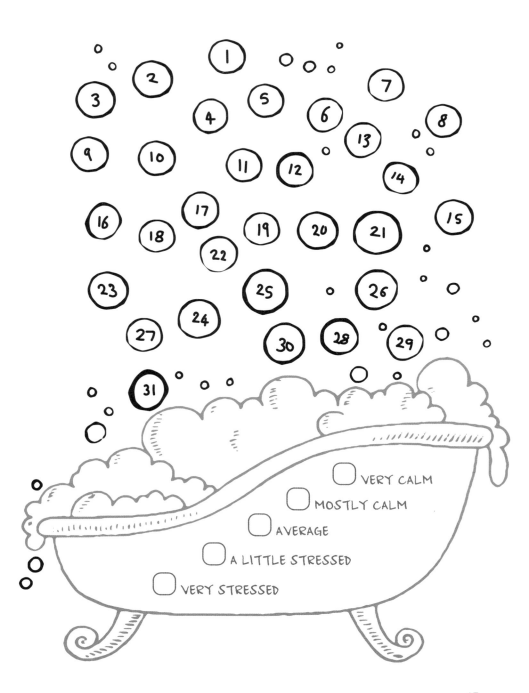

VERY CALM

MOSTLY CALM

AVERAGE

A LITTLE STRESSED

VERY STRESSED

You deserve to feel good as hell.

Lizzo

LISTEN TO YOUR BODY

This is a phrase you've probably heard a lot – but what does it actually mean? How can we listen to our body when it doesn't appear to be talking to us?

The truth is, our body is communicating with us all the time. Take a moment now to stop and pay attention to your breathing; is your breath short and shallow, or steady and deep? Now think about other parts of your body: can you notice any areas of tension or tightness?

It's easy to ignore or not notice the small signs our bodies give us and that could help us to determine what we need.

Try the following body scan exercise, to see if you can tune in to what your body is really feeling.

1   First of all, sit or lie down in a comfortable position, ideally in comfortable and loose-fitting clothes.

2   Close your eyes and, starting with your feet, tune into the sensations you can feel in this area. Are you experiencing any pain or discomfort? Do your feet feel warm or cold?

3   Slowly, move your awareness up from your feet to your lower legs. Again, notice any sensations you might feel.

4   Continue moving your awareness up, body part by body part, until you reach the top of your head.

5   At the end of the exercise, open your eyes, and notice how you feel as a whole.

By repeating this exercise regularly, you'll become much better at listening to your body, and sensing what it needs.

STOP COMPARING

Human bodies are not supposed to look the same, but when the world around us seems to have a "one size fits all" approach to beauty, many of us find ourselves feeling flawed and inadequate.

Comparing ourselves to others might feel natural – even involuntary – but we can all make the choice not to judge ourselves against the appearance (or the success) of others.

Here are some tips to help you break the habit:

♥ **Become aware:** try to catch those thoughts you have when scrolling through social media, or walking down the street; if you find yourself judging someone's attributes in relation to yours, try to acknowledge that feeling, and shift your focus away from it.

- ♥ **Meet yourself:** return to the list of positive attributes you made on p.55 (and make the list longer, if you like). Read through the list, and imagine you were meeting someone with all of these traits for the first time. Can you appreciate yourself in a new light?

- ♥ **Beauty is on the inside:** appearances tell us very little about someone's reality, and you can't judge a person (or how happy they are) from their exterior. Place value in the way someone acts, rather than in the way someone looks.

- ♥ **Celebrate yourself:** nobody is perfect, and it's our diversity that makes us beautiful. Remember that someone else's beauty or brilliance doesn't take away from your own – so celebrate those around you, as well as celebrating yourself!

My body is something that I will NEVER apologize for.

Lili Reinhart

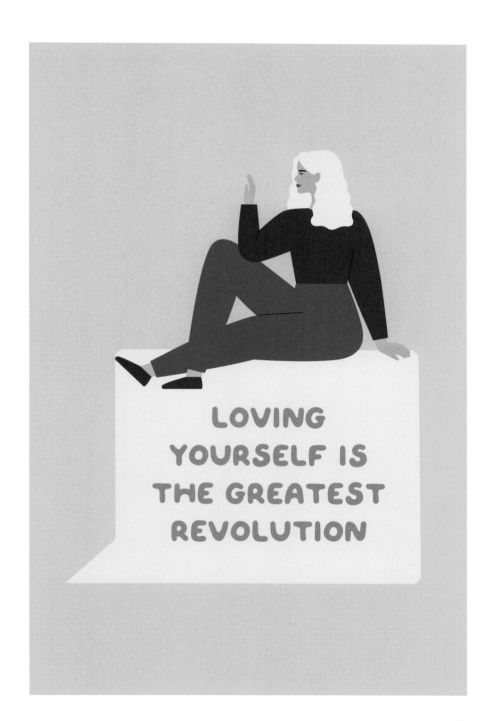

LEARN TO LOVE YOURSELF

This chapter is about learning to love your physical self. Remember that self-love is a journey, and it's not something that you will achieve overnight. Don't be too hard on yourself if you slip up or make mistakes along the way – after all, it's all about progress, not perfection.

Take a moment now to reflect on what you've learned, and then write a letter to your younger self, explaining those key messages. Tell your past self what you have achieved, and what your plans are in the future. Look back on these pages when you need a boost, or when you need a reminder of how far you have already come.

Chapter Four

CHANGING THE RECORD

INTRODUCTION

Changing the script of your life to match your expectations takes time. Many of us have attempted to make rapid changes with strict diets and unachievable New Year's resolutions – only to discover it's near impossible to stick to these unrealistic goals. It's hardly surprising that our enthusiasm quickly fizzles out.

The key is to start with small goals and achieve those, before building up to the bigger challenges. Begin by taking a bird's-eye view of your mindset and habits, and make positive changes to the way you view yourself and how you use your time. By growing your feelings of self-worth and future-proofing your well-being, you'll be better equipped to deal with the big things – whether they're self-imposed goals or the unexpected bumps in the road. This chapter looks at ways to do this, including practising positive self-talk, learning to let go of the things you can't control, and how to form new and lasting habits.

Forming good
habits so they stick

We're all creatures of habit and therefore change is hard, even if our habits are making us miserable. To make a change involves adding something to our lives or taking something away. According to research by psychologists, the best way to make a new habit that sticks is to start small by choosing just one aspect of your life that requires change. It could be spending more time on a creative pursuit – in this instance adding something to your life. This in turn might mean taking something away to find the time for this positive new thing. If you've vowed to spend less time on social media or cooking a full meal night after night (making do with something quick and easy is fine!) then you now have the perfect reason to do so.

Before you embark on any new habit, ask yourself why you want to do it, and make sure it's something you want rather than an idea that you feel you should be doing. Next, seek support and find your tribe – if it's a pastime that others do. Most people are only too pleased to support others and help out. There are many online communities available on social networks too. Celebrate every positive step or breakthrough. And most of all, stick with it! The average habit takes 90 days to form before it becomes a fixed part of your life.

IF YOU ENJOY THE PROCESS, IT'S YOUR DREAM... IF YOU ARE ENDURING THE PROCESS, JUST DESPERATE FOR THE RESULT, IT'S SOMEBODY ELSE'S DREAM.

Salma Hayek

SILENCE YOUR INNER "MEAN GIRL"

Each and every one of us has an inner voice that pipes up to tell us we're not good enough, or deserving, or worthy. When it's particularly loud, it can make it hard to appreciate our achievements, and we somehow think that we are imposters or some terrible mistake has been made and we'll get found out. This can lead us to push ourselves harder, not because we're striving for greater success, but because we're desperate to avoid failure.

The way out of this negative spiral is not to try to obliterate your inner voice, but to reframe your thoughts and rewrite your story as you recount your experiences. When your inner voice is loudly proclaiming that you shouldn't have done that or you're not good enough, try to offset the criticism with positive statements instead. For example, if you don't do so well at a work task, you could say something like, "I am a work in progress. I will try again and I will learn from what has happened before." With practice, this inner critic will evolve into one that is nurturing, supports personal growth and encourages you to seize opportunities that come your way.

What kind things can you say to yourself today? List them here:

Own it, girl!

You are the boss of your destiny, and it's time to take control. Own your thoughts, act on your decisions. Explore your wildest dreams by writing some ideas and hopes in the spaces below.

Think about how you could explore these ideas and make them a reality, and remember to write down the things that might have to go in order to make space for this new reality.

No one can do everything and anything they've ever wanted to do, and throughout your life you will have to compromise not only with others but with yourself too. Finding ways to balance your responsibilities takes time, and it's something you have to actively work on to avoid living the same routine and walking the same path as you've always done.

YOU CAN NEVER LEAVE FOOTPRINTS THAT LAST IF YOU ARE ALWAYS WALKING ON TIPTOE.

Leymah Gbowee

Chapter Five

MOOD MAKERS AND BREAKERS

INTRODUCTION

Our moods are complicated; some days we feel like we could conquer the world, other days we feel like the world has conquered us. This rollercoaster of emotions can affect the way we feel about ourselves, so understanding how we can best manage our moods is an important step in finding happiness.

While we shouldn't forget that low moods are natural – and part of our emotional rhythm – there are usually things we can do to put some pep back into our step.

By learning more about what makes you feel good (and what doesn't), you'll be able to better manage your lifestyle choices, make informed health decisions and avoid triggers that lead to negative moods.

This chapter will explore some of the factors that play into your mood, as well as suggest simple ways that you can boost your happiness. From what you eat to how you sleep – and even who you spend your time with – you'll discover how you can shape your lifestyle to best suit **you**.

It's time to create the life you'll fall in love with!

GOOD FOOD, GOOD MOOD

If you're looking to boost your mood, looking at what you're eating is a great place to start. This isn't about analyzing your every mouthful, but just about being more mindful of how certain foods will make you feel.

Studies have shown that the food we consume affects our mood, and eating a variety of foods rich in minerals, vitamins and fatty acids is essential to living a happy, healthy life.

The following tips will help you to achieve a balanced diet that will improve your mood from the inside out.

Balance blood sugar: if your blood sugar dips too low, you might feel low and irritable. Eat regularly throughout the day (and choose slow-release energy foods, e.g. wholegrain pasta/cereals, rice and nuts) to keep your sugar levels steady.

Eat your EFAs (essential fatty acids): your brain needs EFAs (like omega-3 and -6) to keep it functioning properly. Foods rich in these fatty acids include oily fish, flaxseeds and walnuts.

Stay hydrated: drinking six to eight glasses of water a day is important for our mental health and well-being. Tea, coffee, juices and smoothies all count toward our intake (but try to limit your intake of caffeine and sugar).

Eat the rainbow: we all know we should be eating at least five different fruits and vegetables a day, but we should also bear in mind that we should be eating in full colour (as this will help ensure we consume a good variety of nutrients).

Everything in moderation – the odd biscuit won't hurt (but don't eat the whole packet).

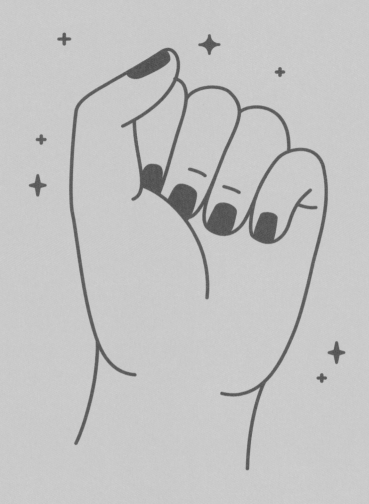

One cannot think well, love well, sleep well, if one has not dined well.

Virginia Woolf

SLEEP WELL, FEEL WELL

It'll likely come as no surprise that being tired can negatively affect your mood. We've all experienced the irritability that comes from a sleepless night, so it makes sense that more sleep means a happier you.

Sleep is the body's way of recharging itself, both physically and mentally, so when you improve the quality of your rest, you might feel better able to take on life's challenges. Seven hours sleep is considered the minimum amount required to remain healthy.

Here are some tips to help you catch those ZZZs:

- **Make your bedroom a sanctuary.** Try to ensure that you keep your room clean, tidy and free from all the sundries of daily life. Opt for soft lighting to create a relaxing atmosphere.

- **Clear your mind:** one of the most common factors in sleep deprivation is worry or stress, so it's important to empty your mind of negative thoughts before you go to bed. You could do this by writing down what's on your mind, or compiling a to-do list for the next day; you could also talk to a friend or loved one about the things that are worrying you.

- **Avoid screens:** the blue light emanating from them can disrupt our body's natural rhythms, so try to put your devices away at least 30 minutes before you go to sleep. Opt for reading a book or a magazine instead, to help you relax before bed.

STOP SCROLLING

Social media has many amazing benefits, and the sense of connection it can bring to our lives is truly valuable. However, there's also a darker side to our social media: the constant comparison with others, the unrealistic standards some people endorse, and the uncontrollable urge we get to endlessly scroll through our feeds night and day.

Research has shown that spending more than 5 hours a day on social media apps can increase symptoms of depression and low self-esteem, so it's important for our mental health that we learn how to control social media, instead of letting it control us.

There's no need to cut social media out of your life altogether (though you may wish to consider cutting down your usage), but you should take a moment to evaluate how you feel after spending time on these apps. If your socials aren't making you happy, try out the following tips.

Curate your feed: keep an eye out for accounts on social media which you smile, teach you something useful or inspire you to live your best life.

Unfollow the negative: if there are people or accounts you follow that make you feel bad about yourself or things in general, remove them! You don't need to give your time or attention to things that bring you down.

Be purposeful: avoid reaching for social media every time you're looking to fill some time. Try to be mindful when you click on your accounts, and think about how you will spend your time on there. Once you've accomplished your aim(s), log out.

Almost everything will work again if you unplug it for a few minutes, including you.

Anne Lamott

DIGITAL MINDFULNESS

Whether your time on social media is productive and positive or not, it's important that you limit the time you spend online. According to a 2019 report by Hootsuite and We Are Social, each of us spends, on average, 6 hours and 42 minutes a day online – that's more than 100 days per year.

Take a moment to think about your own digital usage; perhaps track the time you spend online over the course of a week, to see if you fall above or below this average.

Now consider some of the things you could be doing – which would contribute to your happiness – with all this time. Perhaps you could take up a new hobby, or develop a meditation practice, or join a sports club?

Make a list below of some of the things you would like to try, instead of spending time online:

_____

_____

_____

_____

_____

_____

_____

_____

_____

_____

_____

_____

_____

_____

Learn to say no

If you feel like you're being pulled in every direction, with the demands from work or study, family and social commitments, it can be easy to let yourself slip to the bottom of your to-do list. The fact is, you can't pour from an empty cup – so it's important to make sure you are keeping back enough time to take care of yourself.

Often, we feel that saying no to someone when they ask you a favour makes us a bad person, but this couldn't be further from the truth. If you are taking on everything that comes your way, you are putting your own well-being at risk. If you find that you are taking on too many additional tasks, chores, projects and responsibilities, simply take a step back and consider how that will impact your mental health. If you think that something is going to overwhelm you (or take too much of your time), simply offer a kind but firm response, such as, "Thanks for asking, but I'm afraid I can't."

It's also important to say no to things which – even though you might have the time for them – don't bring you joy, whether it's choosing not to spend time with people who make you feel bad about yourself, or avoiding situations and events that sap too much of your energy. Remember: you don't always have to explain yourself, or offer a detailed excuse. Your time is your own, and you can choose how you spend it.

WHEN YOU SAY "YES" TO OTHERS, MAKE SURE YOU'RE NOT SAYING "NO" TO YOURSELF.

Paulo Coelho

SET YOUR BOUNDARIES

If you need some help in saying no to the things that don't bring you joy, try setting some rules for how you want to spend your time.

First, think about the things that are important to you, and how you want to fit those things into your day. Perhaps you want to make sure you fit in a 20-minute jog before work, or maybe you want to have time to call a loved one every week.

Once you've worked out your priorities, think about how you can make room in your life for them. What rules do you want to set to ensure you fit in the things that make you the happiest? Maybe you want to set yourself stricter working hours, or pledge not to answer emails in the evening, or go to bed at 11 p.m.

Write out ten rules for yourself below. Whenever you are asked to do something which would mean breaking your rules (and thus compromise your well-being), simply say no to it.

1
_____

2
_____

3
_____

4
_____

5
_____

6
_____

7
_____

8
_____

9
_____

10
_____

Chapter Six

WHAT'S REALLY IMPORTANT?

INTRODUCTION

When life seems completely overwhelming, it's so important to take a step back and reflect on what really matters to you.

We live in a society and a culture where we are often expected to meet unrealistic standards of beauty, wealth and career success. If we're not aiming for a promotion at work, toning our bodies, maintaining the perfect skincare regime and setting aside time for a side hustle, we're led to think that we're not doing enough. But how much of all this really brings us happiness?

Though you might find genuine fulfilment at work, or really enjoy going to the gym, the fact is that it's often not the results of these things – the external achievements – that lead to greater happiness. It's not money, or status or a six-pack that ultimately makes you happy, but the relationships you have, and the lifestyle that you lead, and the gratitude you feel for all of those things.

This chapter will help you to take stock of what's really important to you, and suggest ways that you can use to fall back in love with your life.

After all, what's really important is *you*!

Take stock

Before you can start to think about your future, you've got to reflect on your current circumstances. However uncomfortable it might feel, it's important that you take some time to really think about where you are in life, and what you're doing with your time. Think about your job or studies, your home life and your relationships, and consider how much happiness you get from each of them. Be honest!

Once you've taken a moment to think about what you do and what you have, consider what aspects of these things bring you the most joy. Is your work enjoyable and fulfilling, or do you dread going in every day? What about your friends – do they make you feel good about yourself, and do you feel that they would be there for you if you really needed them?

It's easy to live life on autopilot, seeing the same people and doing the same things just because that's what you're used to. But are there things that you could change about your life that would make you happier?

Your happiness should always come at the top of your priority list.

BE HAPPY WITH WHAT YOU HAVE. BE EXCITED ABOUT WHAT YOU WANT.

Alan Cohen

SET GOALS

Once we know what makes us happy in life, we should pursue those things as much as possible. This is why setting goals is so important – not only do they motivate us to turn our dreams into a reality, but even the act of working toward our goals makes us feel more purposeful and (ultimately) more accomplished when we achieve them.

Goals can be short-term, e.g. cooking a new dish every night of the week, or long-term, e.g. writing a book or finding a new job. Whatever your objective, try to make sure that it's something you're willing to commit to, and don't make it so ambitious that it's unlikely you'll achieve it in your desired time frame. For instance, if you want to lift a certain weight at the gym or be able to run a certain distance, think about your current fitness level and draw up a manageable training plan to get to your end goal.

Think about the things that you would love to achieve in the next week, month, year, or more. List some of them below.

REACHING
YOUR GOALS

Now that you've thought about some of
the things you'd like to work toward, it's time
to consider steps you can take to reach them.

To begin, try mapping out the individual steps you will need to
take in order to achieve each goal. If your ambition is fitness-
focused, think about a possible training plan – how many times
a week can you practise, and how much progress would you like
to make in each session? If your goal is financial, think about
setting up a tracker for your income and your expenses,
and consider ways you could reduce your outgoings.

Use the space below to note down some ideas on how
you can attain your goals. Just think about how
satisfying it'll be to work toward something
that's really important to you!

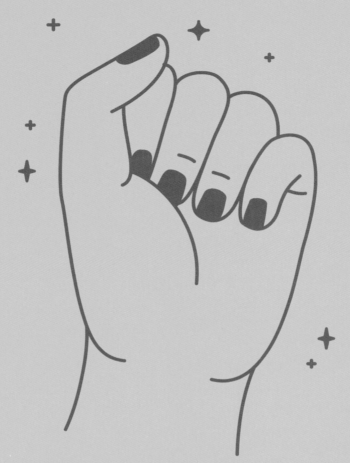

With hard work, with belief, with confidence and trust in yourself and those around you, there are no limits.

Michael Phelps

MANIFESTATION

Having goals and making plans is already a huge step in the right direction to increasing your happiness. But beyond those plans and charts you're making, consider other methods you could explore to help you focus on what matters to you.

A mood board is a big collage of ideas and inspiration, which helps you to develop and manifest your aspirations. It can be digital (on a site like Pinterest) or physical.

As well as providing you with a creative, visual outlet, mood boards are a great way to help you really focus on what you want to achieve, and what you want your life to look like. Plus – frivolous as it all might sound – research by psychologists shows that visualization is much more effective than simply noting down your goals on paper, for helping you reach them.

This phenomenon is generally called "The Law of Attraction", which is the belief that the things you think about can have a direct effect on the outcomes you experience. If, for instance, you go around with a positive mindset and believe that your goals will become a reality, this helps to "attract" those outcomes into your life. If you are faced every day with the visual representation of what you want to achieve, your focus is likely to be much clearer.

Use the next few pages to start planning a mood board. You can write or draw out ideas, or even just list some of the images and words that you'd like to make sure you include.

Your mood board

Use these pages to plan your mood board.

Thoughts become things. If you see it in your mind, you will hold it in your hand.

Bob Proctor

VISUALIZATION MEDITATION

Another way to help your dreams become a reality is to try out visualization techniques. In essence, visualization is like a mental rehearsal of something that you want to achieve. Studies have shown that visualizing a situation or scenario in detail helps you not only to believe that an outcome is possible, but also to improve your focus on it.

Try out the technique below, and come back to this practice whenever you feel like you need a boost of self-belief.

1   Start off by finding a comfortable, quiet space where you can sit, then close your eyes.

2   Take a few moments to find stillness in your body and try to empty your mind.

3   When you feel ready, bring your awareness to your breath. Focus on breathing in through your nose and exhaling through your mouth.

4   After a few deep breaths, conjure an image in your mind, of something that you want to be or achieve. If, for instance, you want to run a marathon, picture yourself running across the finish line. If your goal is to be more compassionate, imagine yourself displaying that behaviour.

5   As you continue to breathe, focus on the details of your pictured scenario. Try to engage with your senses, too. What does the situation you're imagining look like, feel like, sound like?

6   After around 10 minutes – or however long feels good to you – open your eyes, and bring yourself back to the present moment.

Chapter Seven

SELF-CARE FOR EVERY DAY

INTRODUCTION

Repeat after me: "self-care is not selfish".

So often, we find ourselves running around after friends, family and even work colleagues, without giving a second thought to our own well-being. If you really want to help others around you, you've got to meet your own needs first and foremost.

Self-care is about taking the necessary steps to look after your mental, physical, emotional and spiritual well-being. This will mean different things to different people, so it's important that you work out what it is that brings you contentment and calm, and look at how you can make these things a part of your daily routine. Maybe you find relaxation in a lovely hot bubble bath, or perhaps you find that baking bread is therapeutic. Whatever self-care means to you, make it an essential – not an optional – part of your life.

This chapter will offer some practical and easy-to-implement tips and advice for daily self-care. Try each of them out and take on only the things that work for you.

It's time to fall in love with looking after yourself.

SCHEDULE IN "ME TIME"

Sometimes, the best way to commit to a self-care regime is to make it a non-negotiable part of your schedule. After all, you wouldn't diarize a meeting at work or a coffee with a friend and then fail to show up for it – so treat your "me time" the same way!

It doesn't have to be a huge time commitment either – some days it could just be 5 minutes in which you can do something nice for yourself. Whether you enjoy going for a walk and listening to a podcast, eating your lunch mindfully or putting on a face mask before you go to bed, block the time out in your diary and don't be tempted to let everyday chores and responsibilities interfere.

Just by writing down your intentions to commit to self-care – or even by telling others that you will be doing it – you create accountability, which means you are far more likely to follow through with your intentions.

If you can find pockets of time in your diary for "me time", it might also help to write out a short list of ideas for the things you'd like to fill that time with. That way you will always have ideas for your self-care moments, and will be less tempted to spend that time doing something else.

IT'S NOT
SELFISH TO
LOVE YOURSELF,
TAKE CARE OF
YOURSELF AND
TO MAKE YOUR
HAPPINESS A
PRIORITY. IT'S
NECESSARY.

Mandy Hale

SWAP "SHOULD" WITH "COULD"

The words that you use can have a powerful effect on your mindset. Simply by swapping out the word "should" for "could" when talking about your plans you'll find that you feel far less pressure on yourself to do them.

For instance, telling yourself that you "should" go to the gym feels very different from saying that you "could" go to the gym. Suddenly an obligation becomes an option, and you are much more empowered to make an informed choice about it. Maybe you've had a tough day and think that you would rather have dinner and watch your favourite TV show? Maybe you'd like the endorphin release but would rather dance around the living room than spend half an hour on a treadmill?

By making your everyday activities feel less like chores and more like flexible, moveable plans, you might start to feel calmer and more in control of your time. Once you've met any non-moveable deadlines and time commitments, the rest of your diary will open up to far more possibilities – and perhaps you'll discover more time for self-care than ever before.

What's more, by framing your thoughts more positively when it comes to your daily routine, you'll start to feel as though you've made an active choice to go somewhere and do something – and you'll feel even more proud of yourself when you've done it, knowing that you could have easily done something else.

POSITIVE AFFIRMATIONS

Positive affirmations are statements or mantras that you repeat to yourself – out loud or in your head – in order to help improve your mindset and way of thinking. Often, these affirmations reflect the way you want to see yourself, or how you wish to live your life. In addition to the examples peppered throughout this book, you could say something like "I am confident in myself and my abilities"; "I am perfect exactly as I am"; "I choose to live in the present moment"; or "I forgive myself for my past mistakes". Always use the present tense for your affirmations, and try to say them several times a day. Eventually, you will start believing those things are true about yourself, and you'll feel so much happier for it.

Use these pages to jot down some affirmations which you would like to say to yourself. If you need some ideas, simply flick through this book for a wealth of empowerment inspiration!

CHANGE YOUR THOUGHTS AND YOU CHANGE YOUR WORLD.

Norman Vincent Peale

YOGA FLOW

Yoga is a great form of self-care. Not only does it provide us with physical benefits (improving our strength, flexibility and stamina), but it is also fantastic for our minds, helping increase our focus and lower anxiety. With its combination of movement, breathing techniques and meditation, it's great for promoting calm and relaxation.

There are many different styles of yoga, so it's perfect for people of all ages and abilities. Whether you want your yoga to be slow- or fast-paced, gentle or dynamic, explore the different options and find one that suits you.

If you'd like to give yoga a try, here are a few poses to start you off.

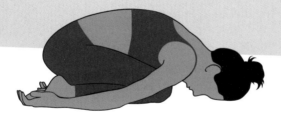

CHILD'S POSE:

Kneel down and, with your knees slightly apart, sit back on your heels. Lean forward to rest your forehead on the ground/mat and rest your arms to your sides. Stay in this pose for as long as it feels good. This is great for a gentle lower back stretch.

DOWNWARD DOG:

This is a classic yoga move. Kneel on all fours with your knees directly below your hips and your hands slightly in front of your shoulders. Spread your fingers, exhale and lift your knees from the floor so you make a triangle shape against the ground. Hold for a few breaths, enjoying the stretch in your hamstrings and lower back.

MOUNTAIN POSE:

Stand up straight with your feet apart. Tighten your stomach and let your arms fall by your sides with palms facing upward. Take several deep breaths.

CONNECT WITH NATURE

Spending time outdoors is something that many of us are doing less and less. With so many digital distractions, and with flexible and remote working becoming increasingly popular, it's easy to spend most of our time inside our own homes. However, going outdoors can have an incredibly restorative effect on both your mind and body. Multiple studies have shown that being out in nature can help to ease stress, fight anxiety and depression, reduce inflammation, improve short-term memory, lower blood pressure, boost your immune system and spark your creativity.

With so many amazing benefits, getting out in the open is a powerful act of self-care. If you're lucky enough to live near woodland, fields or any natural spaces, try to visit them regularly. If you live in a city or a built-up area, try to find a local park, or spend time in a friend's garden (if you don't have your own).

Another benefit of stepping outside on a bright day is the sunshine! As well as making vitamin D directly from being in the sun, your body produces more mood-boosting serotonin, helping you to feel happier and more alert.

Aim for 15 minutes of sunshine with your face, arms and hands exposed to gain maximum benefit. If you're going to be outside in the sun for longer than this, make sure you wear sunscreen with SPF above 15.

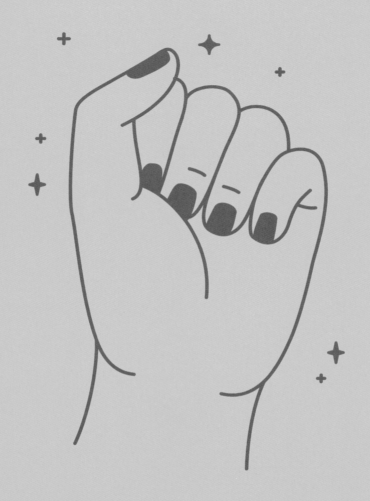

We need the tonic of wildness...
We can never have enough of nature.

Henry David Thoreau

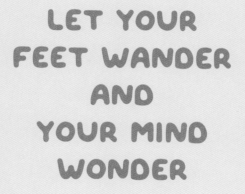

LET YOUR
FEET WANDER
AND
YOUR MIND
WONDER

GRATITUDE

Take a few moments each day to think about the things you are grateful for in your life. Many of us take our blessings for granted – or are simply too busy to even take stock of all the amazing things we have, like our health and our friends, or even our food and shelter.

Use this page to note down all the things you are grateful for. They can be as big or as small as you like! Try to do this a few times a week, and make it a regular habit.

Conclusion

Hopefully, by the time you've reached the end of this book, you'll have already started to fall in love with yourself. If you're not quite there yet: never fear. Self-love is a journey that most of us will be on for a long time – there's simply no quick-fix, snap-your-fingers-and-voilà wizardry to it. But however long it takes, the destination is more magical than anything you can imagine.

Take these tips with you, on your way, and dip in and out of this book as often as you like to restock your toolbox. With any luck, you've uncovered a whole gamut of ideas and exercises that will help you create a life you love.

If you take away one thing from this book, let it be the idea – nay, the firm belief! – that you are absolutely perfect as you are. No matter what anyone tells you (even those pesky voices inside your head), you are exactly where you need to be, and exactly *who* you need to be. Remember that loving yourself isn't about waiting for the perfect incarnation of yourself to form, but about nurturing and valuing yourself on every step along the way.

NOTES

If you're interested in finding out more about our books, find us on Facebook at **Summersdale Publishers**, on Twitter at **@Summersdale** and on Instagram at **@summersdalebooks**.

www.summersdale.com